get ready
get set
GO

a journey to spiritual maturity

get ready
get set
GO

JoAnn Cook

Get Ready, Get Set, Go!
A Journey to Spiritual Maturity

by JoAnn Cook

© 2003, Word Aflame Press
Hazelwood, MO 63042-2299

Cover Design by Paul Povolni

Printed in United States of America

Printed by

WORD AFLAME®PRESS
8855 DUNN ROAD
HAZELWOOD, MO 63042-2299

Library of Congress Cataloging-in-Publication Data

Cook, JoAnn.
  Get Ready, Get Set, Go! : a journey to spiritual maturity / by JoAnn Cook.
    p. cm.
  ISBN 1-56722-618-3
    1. Spiritual life.   I. Title.
  BV4501.3.C663 2992
  248.4—dc21   2002193389

To Timmy and Stephanie
"Friends are the family you choose"

get ready . . .
The Race Begins!

It is our hope that this booklet will provide you, the born again Christian, some direction as you begin your lifetime journey with Jesus Christ. When writing to the Hebrews, the Apostle Paul referred to this journey as a race. He instructed us to run with perseverance the race marked out for us and to fix our eyes on Jesus, the Author and Finisher of our faith (Hebrews 12:1-2). Enjoy each step of your Christian race. Keep your eyes on Jesus and continue running toward the mark He has set for you. Pace yourself to win by applying the principles outlined in these lessons. You will "grow in grace, and in the knowledge of our Lord and Saviour Jesus Christ" (II Peter 3:18) and, with God's help, run this race and cross the finish line in His perfect time.

You're a Christian now, and that means there have been some changes—you're a new creation!

"Therefore if any man be in Christ, he is a new creature: old things are passed away; behold, all things are become new"
(II Corinthians 5:17).

Oh, I know that you look the same. Your shape hasn't changed, and your eyes and hair are still the same color; but a change has happened inside of you. Man is made up of three parts: (1) body, (2) soul, and (3) spirit. Up until the time you became a Christian, you were taking care of your physical body, but now you need to learn how to take care of your spirit and soul. Healthy Christians are spiritually growing Christians. Growth is as normal and necessary for the Christian life as it is for the physical body. Entering God's family by the new birth, believers become "babes in Christ" (I Corinthians 3:1). Regardless of our age, we all begin as spiritual infants needing to "grow up" into our salvation (I Peter 2:2). God wants and expects newborn Christians to grow. To assist us in this spiritual growth, God has given us gifted leaders (Ephesians 4:11-15). Our goal as a new creature in Christ is to become spiritually mature.

Growing spiritually is not automatic; it is a lifelong experience. Maturing in Christ involves many things. Like physical fitness, it includes proper nourishment, adequate exercise, good hygiene, and a positive outlook. Believers need to maintain a balanced spiritual fitness program. This should include the following:

1. Worshiping God
2. Praying
3. Reading the Word of God
4. Listening to the preaching and teaching of the Word
5. Obeying the Word
6. Fellowshiping with like-minded Christians

The following lessons will help you develop your own spiritual fitness. Don't be disappointed if you fail or make mistakes at times—we all do, but you are still loved by God and your brothers and sisters in Christ.

Welcome to His family!

Get Set . . .
Understanding the New Birth

Becoming part of God's family starts with the new birth. When Jesus told Nicodemus that "except a man be born again, he cannot see the kingdom of God" (John 3:3), He meant that everyone must experience a new beginning. Just as human life begins with physical birth, so entry into God's family begins with spiritual birth. God gives a new kind of life, eternal life, to those who have faith in Jesus Christ and trust only in His sacrifice on the cross to reconcile them to God (John 3:16; II Corinthians 5:18; Ephesians 2:8-9). Genuine faith in Christ is expressed not by an intellectual assent that Jesus is Lord, but through obedience to the gospel, that is, through repentance from sin, baptism in Jesus' name, and receiving the gift of the Holy Spirit (Acts 2:38; see I Corinthians 15:1-4). You are a blessed person because you have been born into this new life. Let's take a closer look at what has happened to you.

When you first came in contact with the Spirit of God, you felt His love and His goodness. The Bible says that it is the goodness of God that leads us to repentance (Romans 2:4). Everything in your life began to look and feel different. What once seemed right to you now felt wrong. You became aware of sin in your life and were uncomfortable with it. This spiritual pain and discontentment you experienced is called *conviction*. You were uncomfortable because you knew your life was headed in the wrong direction.

The feeling of conviction led you to repentance. True repentance involves sorrow for sin but primarily consists of a change of mind and direction. You took God's view of sin and, as a result of this new attitude, confessed your sin. Then you made a complete turnaround, walking toward God.

Read I Corinthians 15:1-4, and list the three parts of the gospel (what Jesus did to save us):

(1)_____

(2)_____

(3)_____

Read Acts 2:38, and write down the three things that Peter commanded the crowd to do in order to apply the gospel to their lives (this, of course, is for us also):

(1)_____

(2)_____

(3)_____

The first step in applying the gospel is repentance. When you repented, you renounced your sins and made a decision to turn from them.

Read and write out the following scriptures:

Jeremiah 31:34:

_____
_____
_____

Psalm 103:12:

_____
_____
_____
_____
_____

The second step in applying the gospel is water baptism in Jesus' name. Having repented of your sins, you were baptized by immersion in Jesus' name, by which you identified with the burial of Jesus Christ (Romans 6:3-5) and received the remission of sins.

Give the dictionary definition of the word *remission*.

_____
_____

Read Colossians 2:12, and write it below:

_____

_____

_____

_____

_____

The third step in applying the gospel is receiving the Holy Spirit of God. When you received the gift of His Spirit, you spoke in tongues as the Spirit gave you the ability (Acts 2:1-4; Acts 10:44-46; Acts 19:1-6). This completes the born-again experience.

When you were born again of the water and the Spirit, it is as if you had been created all over again (II Corinthians 5:17). You have a new life! You have now become "dead" to sin (Romans 6:2) and "alive unto God" (Romans 6:11). This new life not only qualifies you for heaven, it also prepares you to experience abundant life in Jesus now (John 10:10). New birth brings growth-enabling changes.

The new birth brings new family relationships.

As a born-again believer, you become a part of "the household of God" (Ephesians 2:19). These new family ties are a special privilege. God becomes your Father. As creator, God fathered all people, but sin cut those family ties (John 8:44). The new birth restores that father-child relationship with God. Those who are born again receive the "right to become children of God" (John 1:12, NIV). With God as their Father, believers rest secure in divine love. They receive love that goes beyond human understanding, and from which nothing can separate them (Romans 8:35-39; Ephesians 3:17-19).

New family support also comes from new brothers and sisters in Christ. The spiritual family includes all those who have obeyed the gospel of Jesus Christ. Fellow believers provide a supportive, caring community that stimulates growth (I Corinthians 12:25-27; Ephesians 4:11-16). God did not plan Christian living to be a solitary experience. Believers need each other. From the birth of the church in Acts 2, Christians have met for worship, instruction, fellowship, prayer, and communion.

Believers learn to apply biblical truth to their everyday lives (Hebrews 5:13-14), to give compassionate support (I Corinthians 12:26), to stimulate each other's faith and, above all, to show brotherly love and hospitality (Romans 12:10-13). The sacrificial love of Christ sets the standard for believers' unselfish love to each other. True Christians are known by their love (John 13:34-35).

Living as a part of God's family cultivates growth. Believers experience healthy self-esteem as they discover that others need them. Each believer has an essential and important contribution to make to the well-being of the church family. Believers grow by giving and receiving help in the family of God.

The new birth brings a change of citizenship.

Ephesians 2:19 tells us that we are no longer strangers, but "fellowcitizens with the saints." Believers now enjoy all the rights and privileges of heavenly citizenship. But this new allegiance creates a problem. Since we continue to be residents of this world, we face the tensions that come from living in a "foreign country." Believers face the challenge of being "in the world," but "not of the world" (John 17:11, 14). Our former home becomes our mission field to win others to Christ (John 17:18). We must live as responsible, law-abiding members of our communities, but without compromising our loyalty to God (Romans 13:1-7).

Newborn believers into God's family also share in a large inheritance.

At the time of your new birth, you received a part of your inheritance. The Holy Spirit, which you received, is a deposit guaranteeing eternal life and spiritual possessions at the second coming of Christ (Ephesians 1:13-14). Like a down payment, the Spirit of God insures the full inheritance at His coming (II Corinthians 5:5).

The Spirit of God produces the fruit of "love, joy, peace, longsuffering, gentleness, goodness, faith, meekness, temperance" (Galatians 5:22-23) in the Christian life. These qualities develop as believers are "filled with the Spirit," which means to allow the Spirit, not the desires of the flesh, to influence your behavior. Growing up as a Christian requires tapping the resources of the Spirit in daily living.

The Holy Spirit is also the mark or "seal" of God's ownership of your life (Ephesians 1:13). New believers recognize the lordship of Jesus Christ. When we confess that Jesus Christ is Lord (Romans 10:9), we are acknowledging Him as our God and Savior. It is not just an outward profession, but an inward, sincere attitude of the heart. Jesus Christ and His Word teach us the lessons of spiritual growth. Christ is our benevolent Master, and we must obey Him. Christ is to be revered as king and given total loyalty and heartfelt worship. Jesus becomes Lord of spiritual matters at home and in the church. He also becomes Lord in intellectual, financial, educational, recreational, vocational—in short—in all areas of life!

What does it mean to you when you say that "Jesus is Lord"?

_____

_____

_____

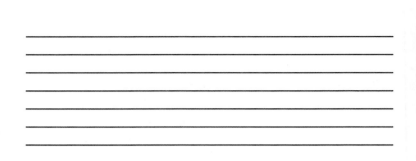

Summary

An important goal for all Christians is spiritual maturity. Reaching spiritual maturity is an ongoing process whereby you grow toward a deeper understanding of the Christian life and of Jesus Christ Himself. The first step to this process is understanding the new birth. It is important to realize that you now have a new family with whom to relate, a new citizenship to be respected, and a new inheritance to enjoy.

Vital to spiritual growth is the recognition of Jesus Christ as Lord in every aspect of your life. The recognition of His lordship will lead you toward a deeper understanding of Christ and farther down the road toward spiritual maturity.

Go! . . .
Growing in Our Relationship with Jesus Christ

It is very important that we perceive Christianity as more than a religion—but as a relationship with Jesus Christ. Growing in our relationship with Jesus involves personal and progressive commitment. Personal commitment because it involves you; progressive commitment because it is dynamic and continues to grow and change as you do. It is a commitment because it involves giving yourself. Our relationship with Him involves discipleship.

Discipleship comes from the word *discipline*, and Jesus has called us to spiritual discipline: spiritual training designed to produce character and behavior patterned after Jesus Christ. A disciple is both a learner and a follower. We devote time to learning about Him and from Him, and as a result, we willingly follow His ways. There are several important disciplines in the Christian life:

(1) Reading and studying the Word of God provides us with the knowledge, inspiration, and encouragement that we need every day. The Bible is the resource for consistent Christian living, and we should read it with intense personal interest. The ultimate purpose of studying Scripture is to relate biblical truth to daily living and to become "doers of the word" (James 1:22).

Take time to read the Bible every day. Jesus said, "Man shall not live by bread alone, but by every word that proceedeth out of the mouth of God" (Matthew 4:4). It is a good idea to keep a notebook of things you learn. Try to concentrate on one verse and think about it all day. When you read, pray that God will help you understand what you read. God's Holy Spirit lives in you, and since He inspired the writing of the Bible, He understands it. Ask Him to reveal the Word to you.

If you are not sure where to start reading the Bible, start with the four Gospels of the New Testament (Matthew, Mark, Luke, and John). By reading these books, you will learn about Jesus: His words and deeds. Next, read the Acts of the Apostles and experience the faith and excitement that results when the teachings of Jesus are put into action! Then read the Epistles and learn how to have a victorious life in Christ. Finally, read the Book of Revelation, and see the ultimate victory of God as John did. When you have read the New Testament, then read the Old Testament. The lessons and history of the Old Testament are rich indeed, and provide essential background information for the New Testament.

Determine in yourself to hide the Word of God in your heart by memorizing verses every week. Such an attitude and practice will keep you from temptation and failure. The psalmist knew this when he wrote, "Thy word have I hid in mine heart, that I might not sin against thee" (Psalm 119:11).

(2) Daily communication with God. Very early in the life of a child, he learns to communicate with his parents. The first attempt may be a certain kind of cry, sound, or facial expression. No one but the parent is able to understand these attempts at speech. The born-again Christian will also learn to communicate with his heavenly Father. This is done through prayer.

When you pray, realize that God has shown us by His actions and words that He is a warm and personal Father. Jesus assured us that He cares and urges us to pray (Matthew 7:7-11). Encouraged by His divine love, we can confidently speak to Him every day. When you pray, talk to God in the same manner as you would talk to your own father, respected friend, or advisor. You will find that He is interested in the daily problems that you face. These first attempts at prayer may be awkward, but this doesn't matter. God listens to your heart's cry. He is able to understand your very thoughts.

Without a doubt, prayer is one of the most vital elements in your walk with God. It is good to have a certain time to pray. You do not want to be casual about your prayer life, praying only when it is convenient. When you pray that way, you lack earnestness and effectiveness. God wants to be the most important one in your daily schedule. If you learn to put God first while you are still a young Christian, the conflicts ahead will be much easier.

Prayer encourages an intimate relationship between you and God. You will learn to sense His presence. Prayer does make a difference.

Look up James 5:16, and write it in your own words:

_____

_____

_____

_____

_____

_____

_____

Prayer should include worship. When believers clear their minds of the clutter from daily life and focus on God's presence, a feeling of love and warmth fills their hearts, and you can't help but adore Him for who He is and for what He has done for you. When we begin to worship God and recognize His holiness, then confession will come naturally as part of our prayer.

Daily confession is an integral part of healthy prayer. When we accept God's mercy and forgiveness, it brings spiritual growth.

Read I John 1:9, and write the passage in your own words:

_____

_____

_____

_____

_____

_____

Thanksgiving is an important aspect of prayer. Having received God's forgiveness and sustaining strength, we feel a deep sense of gratefulness. Thanksgiving is an attitude that produces spiritual balance.

Read I Thessalonians 5:18, and write it below:

_____

_____

_____

_____

_____

_____

Even experiences that normally cause tension can be faced with thankful prayer anticipating inward peace (Philippians 4:6-7). Knowing that God is in control and will use this hardship to promote spiritual growth is adequate reason to pray thankfully (Romans 8:28; James 1:2-4).

Prayer is also a time to ask God to meet the needs of others. This kind of prayer is called *intercession*. Through prayer you can contribute positively to the lives of others far beyond the limits of your personal resources and capacities (Philippians 1:19).

Finally, prayer is telling God all the details of everything that concerns you. Read Philippians 4:6 and paraphrase it:

_____

_____

_____

_____

_____

Seeking help from God for personal challenges, problems, and opportunities is not selfish. Jesus encouraged His disciples to take their requests to God in His name (John 16:23-24). Through prayer you receive divine help for your daily needs.

Prayer has always played a vital part in the lives of God's people. Old Testament leaders Abraham, Moses, Nehemiah, Elijah, Elisha, and David all witnessed God's direct involvement in their lives through prayer. As a man, Jesus prayed regularly to His heavenly Father. Following His example and teaching, the apostles, and later the early church, placed priority on prayer. In all these situations, God followed no single pattern in responding to people's requests. Whether the loving answer was "yes," "wait," or "no," prayer still made a difference in their lives.

Prayer continues to be an effective force in the modern world. Although many non-Christians in this scientific age deny supernatural intervention in daily events, evidence abounds that God still answers prayer. Testimonies surround you of God's faithful answers to the requests of His children. If doubt begins to enter your mind, just ask your brothers and sisters at your church to share their answers to prayer with you.

As new Christians, it is easy to become frustrated when we do not see direct results from our prayers. We may even be prone to accuse God of not keeping His word, when in reality, we have misunderstood His promises concerning prayer. Prayer is a request for help, not a demand for action. God evaluates every prayer by His infinite wisdom and unfailing goodness, and then He gives only what He knows is best. Be assured of this.

From our limited human perspective, disease, hardships, adversity, and persecution seem totally negative. Given the option, we would all veto having these experiences invade our lives. Yet these problems are part of the sinful, fallen world in which we live out our Christian faith. Knowing that we can rely on prayer promises helps us to maintain a balanced perspective while we are in the middle of difficulties.

Write down the following prayer promises:
I John 5:14-15:

_____
_____
_____
_____

Ephesians 3:20:

_____
_____
_____
_____
_____

Romans 8:28:

_____
_____
_____
_____
_____

God promises to come to the aid of His children in hard circumstances, but never did He promise to exempt them from such hardships. In fact, Jesus warned His disciples that they would have tribulation in this world, and He offered peace in the crisis, not immunity from it (John 16:33). God sometimes chooses to glorify His name by miraculously removing the problem. At other times, He strengthens believers so that they can persevere to God's glory. Anytime God chooses not to heal sickness or to remove difficult circumstances, His children can rest in confident assurance that God will give some better spiritual benefit.

Recognize prayer as a powerful force in your life, and practice it continuously.

(3) Fasting is a spiritual discipline that is good to begin practicing early in your walk with God. Fasting is taught throughout the Old and New Testaments as a method of releasing our faith to believe God, of giving power to our prayers, and of bringing our body into subjection to the Spirit. There are many types of fasts in the Bible, and you should learn and practice them. If you have questions about different types of fasting, contact your pastor or another minister in your church who will explain any details you may not fully understand. Our church will often designate a weekly day of fasting. In addition to our regular weekly fast day, we will, from time to time, request a designated fast to meet special or urgent needs.

During a day of fasting, our main objective is to devote ourselves to prayer and to give ourselves entirely to God.

Read Isaiah 58:6-12, and write in your own words the results of prayer when combined with fasting:

_____

_____

_____

_____

_____

Jesus gave further instructions for fasting in Matthew 6:16-18.

(4) Faithful attendance to church services is another important discipline that promotes rapid spiritual growth. The writer of the Book of Hebrews charged us:

"And let us consider one another
to provoke unto love and to good works:
not forsaking the assembling of ourselves
together, as the manner of some is;
but exhorting one another: and so much
the more, as ye see the day approaching"
(Hebrews 10:24-25).

Worshiping the Lord together with your brothers and sisters is an important source of spiritual nourishment. Attending services gives us the opportunity to hear the Word of God preached and taught, giving us direction for our daily life. God speaks to our heart and increases our faith through the preached word.

Read Romans 10:17 and summarize it:

_____

_____

_____

_____

_____

_____

We develop stability in our lives by knowing the Word of God. In addition to hearing the Word, church attendance provides us with an opportunity to share our gifts with others and to minister to them. It is through giving and receiving that we grow in God.

(5) Telling others about the good news of the gospel is called *witnessing*. Acts 1:8 says, "Ye shall receive power, after that the Holy Ghost is come upon you: and ye shall be witnesses." The power to witness comes to everyone who is filled with the Spirit. To witness is simply to relate your experience to others, telling them what God has done in your life. A witness only tells about what he knows. Relate to others how the gospel of Jesus Christ has transformed your life. You will be surprised how easy it is to become an effective witness for Jesus Christ. The more you talk about what God has done, the stronger you will become in the Spirit. It is truly a paradox: the more you give, the more you will receive!

(6) Giving of our finances and of ourselves is a spiritual discipline and an act of worship that brings many blessings to the life of a believer. We want to be generous right from the beginning of our Christian walk. As Christians, we learn to give freely from the heart, for "God loveth a cheerful giver" (II Corinthians 9:7). The Bible speaks of giving our tithe and offerings.

Read Malachi 3:8-10, and write it in your own words:

_____

_____

_____

_____

_____

The tithe is ten percent of our earnings, and it is designated for the support of the ministry and the spreading of the gospel message. Offerings include many areas of giving over and above the tithe.

The promises of God are in the Word to encourage us to give. Read Luke 6:38, and write it below:

_____

_____

_____

_____

_____

In addition to giving of your substance, you will want to give of yourself and become involved in the family of God. Instead of being a bystander, make yourself available to do whatever is needed. Volunteer your services with a free and willing heart, and you will be truly blessed with growth beyond measure!

Summary

Growing in our relationship with God involves certain spiritual disciplines. We are becoming disciples of Jesus Christ growing closer to Him day by day. We realize the importance of becoming "doers of the word" by praying, reading the Scripture, fasting, attending church faithfully, witnessing, and giving of ourselves freely and generously. Our spiritual growth will be dependent on how we apply these disciplines. Our first steps with the Lord are simple ones, but they are vital to maturity. The Christian life is a forward progression, a growing-up process. By following God's Word, we will reach our goal of spiritual maturity.

Living a Christian Lifestyle

Christians who desire to grow spiritually will only impact the people who surround them when they live what they say they believe. Holiness is not an option for the growing Christian; it is part of our service in the kingdom of God.

Holiness is not just living up to some superficial human standard of perfection. Holiness is an attitude of the heart that expresses itself in godly living. In order to establish such a holy lifestyle, you must first focus on cultivating a heart for God. Then, work on overcoming temptations in your life; and, finally, establish patterns of holy living.

Cultivate a heart for God.

The word *heart* in the Bible describes the whole inner life of an individual: the mind, emotions, and will. Being filled with the Spirit and led by the Spirit overflows into words, actions, and godly behavior. A godly lifestyle flows from a heart filled with the Spirit of God.

God has never been satisfied with worship and service that is "put on" like you would put on a coat or a hat. Such religious activity is futile unless it comes from the heart. God has commanded us to love Him with our whole being: heart, soul, mind, and strength

(Deuteronomy 6:5; Matthew 22:37). God wants us to have hearts that are open to His guidance. Once you, as a growing Christian, have opened your heart to God, you learn to daily examine yourself and confess any known sin. This practice keeps the Spirit of God alive and working in us. In the Old Testament, David confessed his sin and was called "a man after God's own heart."

Overcome temptation.

All Christians are susceptible to temptation. There are three practical ways you can overcome temptation.

1. Admit your weaknesses. Some believers, in a feeble attempt to keep a good image in front of others, act as if they never struggle with sin or temptation. They often feel that, if they share their struggles, they will appear "weak." Actually, quite the opposite is true. Hebrews 11:34 tells us that the Bible heroes "out of weakness were made strong." II Corinthians 12:7-10 says that His "strength is made perfect in weakness." The power of the Holy Spirit is activated in believers' lives when they are humbly aware of their own weaknesses. Keeping a humble heart before God helps us overcome temptation.

2. Use God's resources. The power of God is unleashed when you humbly depend on Him for

strength in the middle of your human weakness. God's resources are available for you to overcome temptation. Paul referred to some of God's resources as the "armour of God." He challenged us to arm ourselves with the Word and persistent prayer.

Read Ephesians 6:10-20, and summarize these verses:

_____

_____

_____

_____

3. Guard your thought life. Sin comes from the heart, so any strategy to overcome temptation begins with the heart. When Christians fall, it is usually because they have allowed sinful thoughts and desires to burn unrestrained in their hearts over a period of time. The way to overcome such temptation is to learn to discipline thoughts.

Paul explained to us how he avoided falling into Satan's schemes: "[Bring] into captivity every thought to the obedience of Christ" (II Corinthians 10:5). For us to continue to grow and mature in Christ, we need to guard our heart from any thought or desire that would violate scriptural principles or laws.

By dealing ruthlessly with sin at the thought level, you are more likely to refrain from sinful actions. At the first indication of a tempting thought, meditate on an appropriate scripture, or sing a song of praise. By drawing your thoughts toward God, you will receive deliverance from temptation.

Establish a pattern of holy living.

To continue to grow as a Christian, your lifestyle needs to become consistent with all biblical principles of holiness. While establishing a godly lifestyle begins in the heart, it is evidenced by daily behavior. Godly actions and deeds come from a pure heart and a disciplined lifestyle.

God instructs us to be holy because He is holy. Read I Peter 1:15-16, and write the verses down:

_____

_____

_____

_____

As a growing Christian, you should strive to live up to God's standard of holiness, which is found in His Word. This is a natural and heartfelt response to His mercy and grace.

Read Romans 12:1-2 and summarize it:

_____

_____

_____

_____

_____

The key to holy living is the total commitment of your whole self to serving God. Rather than conforming to the standards and lifestyle of the world, conform to biblical standards of behavior. Your mind will reflect the thoughts and desires of the mind of Christ. As you allow your lifestyle to be transformed by the mind of Christ, you will become a living example of God's will.

What is the evidence in your life that God's Spirit is transforming your . . .

thoughts?

_____

_____

_____

_____

actions?

_____
_____
_____
_____

speech?

_____
_____
_____
_____
_____

attitudes?

_____
_____
_____
_____

appearance?

_____
_____
_____
_____
_____

relationships?

_____

_____

_____

_____

habits?

_____

_____

_____

_____

goals?

_____

_____

_____

_____

As a Christian, you will recognize the importance of
discipline in all areas of your life—social, mental, emotional, physical, and moral—to achieve a healthy balance. Regular social activities are enjoyable and will
encourage friendships in the family of God. Set goals
for yourself concerning intellectual development. This

could mean setting up a regular pattern of stimulating reading, Bible studies, or enrolling in classes or seminars.

Guard your emotional life so that neither past experiences nor present pressures monopolize your time or energy. Find healthy ways to express your emotions through wholesome friendships, recreation, and hobbies. Keeping in shape physically through a regular exercise program and a healthy diet has a great effect on both emotional and spiritual health.

As a growing Christian, you must maintain strict discipline on the moral and ethical areas of your life. Sexuality, power, and money pose serious moral temptations. A daily time of prayer and personal reflection will help you stay in tune with God. In addition, as a growing, maturing believer, make yourself accountable on a deep interpersonal level to at least one other godly Christian outside your immediate family. This individual is to be someone who will encourage you in holy living and who will stay with you as you struggle in your "striving against sin" (Hebrews 12:4). This will help you to maintain spiritual equilibrium.

Summary

Evidence of spiritual growth is the daily living of a godly lifestyle. To establish a godly lifestyle, we cultivate a heart for God by being open to His guidance, confessing known sin, being filled with the Holy Ghost, overcoming temptation, and establishing a pattern for holy living.

Developing Personal Relationships

The Bible emphasizes that it is important for growing Christians to develop right relationships within their family, church, and the world. The success of Christians in growing toward spiritual maturity depends, to a great extent, on their ability to relate positively to other people.

The Bible provides solid reasoning for Christians to develop positive relationships with other people. This reasoning includes (1) the nature of fellowship, (2) the nature of the church, and (3) the command of Jesus Christ.

The word *fellowship* comes from the Greek word *koinonia*, which literally means a sharing together, participation, or common ownership. When it is used within the context of believers, it refers to the intimate relationship that believers share with Jesus Christ and with one another. These two relationships are closely linked in Scripture. I John 4:11-12 illustrates this connection:

> *"Beloved, if God so loved us,*
> *we ought also to love one another.*
> *No man hath seen God at any time.*
> *If we love one another, God dwelleth in us,*
> *and his love is perfected in us."*

The biblical concept of "fellowship" encourages Christians to care deeply for one another out of their common loyalty to Jesus Christ. The church, by definition, is a body of believers joined together by their common commitment to Jesus Christ. As a body, the church is held together by the proper relationships of its members to one another (Ephesians 4:16). The growth of the church depends on how well all members use their gifts and talents to serve, encourage, and develop other people.

Growing Christians want to work diligently at developing loving relationships with other people simply because Jesus commanded it: "A new commandment I give unto you, That ye love one another; as I have loved you, that ye also love one another" (John 13:34). Jesus not only commanded His followers to love one another, but He showed them how to do it. When Jesus told His disciples to love others as He had loved them, He knew exactly what He was saying. He had spent His life modeling in very concrete ways what love was all about.

Family relationships

Good family relationships are basic to developing relationships within the church and world. One of the most significant indicators of a healthy family is a good relationship between husband and wife. When the Bible deals with family issues, it begins with this relationship (Ephesians 5). If you are married, as a growing Christian, give priority to your spousal relationship and work diligently to develop it. Couples need to plan mutually enjoyable activities with each other and never be too busy for one another. Pray together. Talk together. Work together. Dream together. Special times like these are essential in building warmth and trust in this top-priority relationship. If your spouse is not walking with God, it is all the more reason for you to keep your relationship a priority. Your godly lifestyle and kind spirit will be the message they respond to. Do not be tempted to push your spouse into a relationship with God. Let it be their choice, in their time.

It is also a temptation for many Christians to get so involved in ministry that they neglect their children. In the case of younger Christians, the tendency may be to draw away from parents they still live with. It is important that we be sensitive to the needs of our family. Relationships take time to build, and children need to have plenty of time to spend with their parents if they are to assimilate the biblical values that the parents hold. The quality of the relationship between parent and child often determines whether or not the child follows the biblical values held by their parents.

Growing Christians need to invest whatever time necessary to develop quality relationships with their family members.

Church relationships

Growth within the church is dependent upon the quality of relationships between believers. Believers are challenged to edify, confess faults to, empathize with, submit to, and accept one another.

To edify means to build up and strengthen one another. We do this primarily by encouraging one another (Romans 14:19; I Thessalonians 5:11). This skill is important, particularly if you wish to become involved in any type of ministry. The primary skill needed to motivate others is the ability to support and encourage. Learn and practice this skill as a new Christian.

A sign of growing Christians is their ability to confess sin and weakness. By readily acknowledging mistakes, you show others that you are teachable and humble. Like all Christians, you will make mistakes and grow from the experience. Confessing faults before God and to others will keep you accountable to the body of Christ (James 5:16).

Growing Christians need to empathize or identify with the feelings of other people. Paul challenged us to "regard one another as more important than himself; do not merely look out for your own personal interests, but also for the interests of others" (Philippians 2:3-4, NASB). In sorrow, bear the emotional burdens of other believers (Galatians 6:2). In the middle of another's joy, celebrate (Romans 12:15)!

The mutual submission that is taught in the Word of God (Ephesians 5:21) implies that believers learn to be sensitive to the needs of others. It suggests that we listen carefully to their ideas and thoughts. If you want to continue to grow and mature in Christ, you need to develop an attitude of humble respect for all people.

The church of Jesus Christ is a combination of men, women, and children from various cultures, nationalities, traditions, languages, and political persuasions. Inevitably there will be, from time to time, tensions and barriers based upon these differences. Yet, in spite of these differences, the church is by nature a unified body. Members should accept one another for who and what they are right now. As a growing Christian, you will want to avoid the temptation to work only with those with whom you share common interests. Instead, go out of your way to develop closer relationships with people from many backgrounds.

Relationships within the world

One of the real tests of your spirituality will be your ability to relate to people in the world while maintaining your Christian witness. The church is to fulfill the great commission, in large part, by developing relationships with non-Christians. Yet in drawing close to people who have opposing values and lifestyles, we should be careful not to become conformed to these.

Jesus spent a great deal of His time building relationships with people who were considered the worst of sinners. Yet He was able to develop these relationships without being affected by their ungodly values. We should follow His example. Be careful not to get so wrapped up in activities that you have no time or energy left to develop relationships with non-Christians. It is vital to the growth of God's church to maintain a balance in your personal relationships between Christians and non-Christians.

Friendship evangelism was the approach of Jesus. It is based upon building relationships with non-Christians in normal daily contacts. Within such relationships, we look for opportunities to demonstrate love and share our faith. As a growing Christian, learn to ask appropriate questions, listen, empathize, and tactfully bring in the gospel message at the right time. Learn to be able to maintain friendships with non-Christians in spite of their apparent apathy towards spiritual things. Put a high priority on building personal relationships with people without compromising your own biblical views and standards. Jesus did this, and many people were enlightened. We can follow His example.

Problems with people

Where there are people, there are problems. The church is no different. Christians are not perfect people. As you grow spiritually, prepare yourself to deal with problems in relationships by learning to forbear and forgive.

Christians have personality weaknesses, bad habits, annoying mannerisms, and personal struggles (just like everyone else). If we, as growing Christians, want to have a positive influence on people, we will learn to be patient with offensive people.

Look up Ephesians 4:1-3, and paraphrase the verses:

_____

_____

_____

_____

_____

_____

Christians learn to "put up" with many of the offensive behaviors of others. In the process of maturing, most sincere Christians will put off behaviors that are offensive and put on behaviors more consistent with the fruit of the Spirit. The first response of the maturing Christian to another who may "rub you the wrong way" is that of patient forbearance.

To be a mature and effective Christian, guard your heart from bitterness or resentment. Read Ephesians 4:31-32, and paraphrase the verses:

_____

_____

_____

_____

Inevitably, you will be hurt or offended by someone in the course of your Christian experience. Be careful how you deal with your hurt feelings. Remember, some offensive behavior can be ignored and forgotten. Other behavior needs to be tactfully confronted. If people sincerely ask for forgiveness, the problem usually takes care of itself. However, if someone refuses to accept responsibility for their offense, or blames another, the problem will usually get worse. At this point, you may be tempted to hold bitter feelings. The appropriate response is to forgive that person.

In Matthew 18:22, when Peter asked Jesus how many times he should forgive a person who offended him, Jesus said:

_____

_____

_____

_____

Growing Christians should be willing to forgive any person who hurts them so that bitterness does not take root in their heart.

Summary

We are responsible, as growing Christians, to develop skills in relating to our family, our church, and the world around us. We want to spend priority time with our spouses and children. In our relationships with people in the church, we learn to develop skills in edifying, confessing faults, empathizing, submitting, and accepting others. In our relationships with people in the world, we want to follow Jesus' example by developing friendships with non-Christians, while being careful not to be conformed to their non-Christian values. We also will learn to develop the ability to deal with relationship problems through forbearing and forgiving others.

Discovering Your Place of Service

One of the first discoveries you will make as a growing Christian is that you are saved to serve. You are not saved simply to satisfy yourself. Jesus Christ saves you in order that He may use you in His plan for ministry here in this present world. You have received a unique privilege of serving the Most High God! Jesus said, "Ye have not chosen me, but I have chosen you, and ordained you, that ye should go and bring forth fruit" (John 15:16).

Jesus has chosen to delegate specific ministry tasks to all believers. To accomplish this ministry, He has given each one of us special gifts to benefit others and to glorify God.

Study the following outline to better understand the ministry gifts as presented in the Word of God. Look up and read the corresponding scriptures:

  I. God intends that believers be wise concerning spiritual gifts (I Corinthians 12:1).
  A. They are gifts (Romans 1:11).

  B. They are given by the Holy Spirit to enable the believer to serve.

 II. Every child of God has one or more gifts (I Corinthians 12:7).

III. Personal gifts serve a unique purpose (Ephesians 4:11-12).

IV. Gifts make believers accountable to God (I Timothy 4:12,14).

V. Gifts are different from natural talents (I Peter 4:11).

VI. Three categories of spiritual gifts:
   A. The supernatural gifts (I Corinthians 12:1-11)
      1. Word of wisdom
      2. Word of knowledge
      3. Gift of faith
      4. Gifts of healing
      5. Gift of working of miracles
      6. Gift of prophecy
      7. Discerning of spirits
      8. Gift of tongues
      9. Gift of interpretation of tongues

   B. The services gifts
      1. Gift of helps (I Corinthians 12:28) - the ability to serve the church in any supportive role.
      2. The gift of hospitality (Romans 12:13; I Peter 4:9) - the special ability to provide an open house and warm welcome for all people.
      3. The gift of giving (Romans 12:8) - the

delightful donation to the cause of Christ.

4. The gift of government (I Corinthians 12:28) - the special gift of leadership, lay or ministerial.
5. The gift of mercy (Romans 12:8) - the gift of empathy and action toward the needy.
6. The gift of exhortation (Romans 12:8) - the gift of encouraging and comforting others.
7. The gift of teaching (Romans 12:7; Ephesians 4 :11) - the special ability to explain and apply the Word of God.

C. The ministry gifts (Ephesians 4:11)
1. Apostles
2. Prophets
3. Evangelists
4. Pastors/Teachers

The big question for new Christians is this: "Which gifts do I have?" This is a question you will answer for yourself as your spiritual life grows. Use the following guidelines prayerfully to assist you in determining your area of giftedness:

1. Discover your strengths. The first step in determining your spiritual gifts is to try to discover your strengths. Be careful to screen out those strengths or successes that are most likely due to your own talent or learned skills. What you need to discover here are those victories and successes that seem to go beyond

natural explanation. Think about those successful events that can only be attributed to some supernatural source. Discovering these events will be a key to your spiritual gifts.

2. Discover your weaknesses. Following the above strategy, evaluate why other events seemed not to work out well as you attempted to minister. When you uncover these failures, areas of ineffectiveness, or weaknesses in your ministry attempts, a pattern will emerge that will reveal those gifts which God has not given you.

3. Consult Christian friends. To gain further insight, it is helpful to consult with mature believers whom you know well and who have observed you during times when you have been ministering. These believers are individuals who will be comfortable sharing with you objectively and truthfully.

4. Use the process of trial and error. In pursuit of your spiritual gifts, some trial and error will be necessary. The Scripture says, "Try the spirits whether they are of God" (I John 4:1). You will need to make many attempts at ministry to find a revealing pattern that will enable you to focus on the gifts that will best benefit the kingdom of God.

Once your ministry gifts have been determined, the next step is personal commitment. These are your gifts, and God holds you accountable to use them. Using your gifts becomes a high priority. They are part of God's divine plan for your ministry in the church.

After you discover your gifts, part of your commitment is to develop them. When you receive your gifts from the Lord, they are usually somewhat primitive and in need of considerable development and usage in order to make them as effective as He wants them to be. This is an ongoing process—a lifetime education.

Read I Timothy 4:14-16 and summarize:

_____
_____
_____
_____
_____
_____
_____

Make it a point as a new Christian to desire spiritual gifts, to pray for them, to discover them, and to utilize them for the kingdom of God. Jesus said, "I must be about my Father's business" (Luke 2:49). This statement applies to every maturing Christian as well. Christians who become active in their personal ministry become victorious in their walk with Jesus Christ and are not as prone to failure, discouragement, or disillusionment.

Summary

Discovering your spiritual gifts is a very important part of your continued maturing in Jesus Christ. By using your Spirit-given gifts in ministry to others, you are contributing to the body of Christ and glorifying God! The varieties of gifts outlined in the Bible are an indication of the diversity of people's needs. A prayerful examination of your life and consultation with mature believers will help you to discover your gifts. After discovering your gifts, you will want to develop them and use them in service for our sovereign God.

I Am Making Progress

One gauge of your spiritual progress and maturity is the spiritual fruit produced in your life by the Holy Spirit. Galatians 5:19-25 describes the works of the flesh as well as the fruit of the Spirit. Look up this passage of Scripture and define:

The works of the flesh are:

_____

_____

_____

_____

_____

_____

_____

_____

_____

_____

_____

_____

_____

The fruit of the Spirit is:

_____

_____

_____

_____

_____

_____

_____

_____

Now make a list of the fruit of the Spirit that you see developing in your life:

_____

_____

_____

_____

_____

_____

_____

Make a list of the works of the flesh that were once a part of your life but are no longer a part of it:

_____

_____

_____

_____

_____

_____

_____

_____

See, you are making progress! The works of the flesh are disappearing, and the fruit of the Spirit is growing! Don't be disappointed if you see some things in your life that still need changing. Maturity does not come overnight. Gradually, with God's help, you will become more and more like Jesus Christ. The works of the flesh need to be pruned or cut off because they sap us of the spiritual nutrition we need to produce good fruit. If the works of the flesh are still being produced after we have become a Christian, it is a sign that we are still allowing the roots of our old nature to exist. We need to allow God's Spirit within us to prune off these branches and sever their tap-root. Pray and ask God to help you cultivate the fruit of the Spirit and not the works of the flesh. Be patient, remember that God loves you, and know that you are growing in Him!

Summary

Growing Christians cultivate the fruit of the Spirit in their lives. It is a gauge of maturity. Jesus said, "Wherefore by their fruits ye shall know them" (Matthew 7:20). What a person really is, is far more important than what he says. Fruit-bearing is a life-changing and lifelong process. Be patient and keep growing in Christ!

Conclusion

We all share in the excitement of your new birth experience. You have chosen to run in this Christian race, leading to true peace, happiness, and eternal life. By pacing yourself, you will gain spiritual maturity . . . one step at a time.

It is our hope that you feel welcomed, loved, and needed in your new family, the family of God. One of the best ways to gain knowledge and understanding of the Word of God and your new life in Christ is to participate in a ten-week home Bible study program entitled "Search for Truth" or a twelve-week study entitled "Exploring God's Word." When you have completed that study, enroll in a discipleship class if one is offered at your church. In the small group atmosphere of the class, you will feel comfortable to ask questions and to participate in discussions, which will enhance your experience. If there is not a discipleship class at your church, ask your pastor or another minister in your church for direction in the selection of reading material to guide you in your growth as a disciple of Jesus Christ.

Your church ministerial staff will always be available to assist you in any way they can. Get ready, get set, go! We are all running this race together!

"Being confident of this very thing, that he which hath begun a good work in you will perform it until the day of Jesus Christ" (Philippians 1:6).

"For we are his workmanship, created in Christ Jesus unto good works, which God hath before ordained that we should walk in them" (Ephesians 2:10).